Becoming Proficient in NLP Transformers:

A Beginner's Guide to Developing, Training, and
Elevating State-of-the-Art Language Models with
Practical Guidance and Strategies

Matthew D.Passmore

.

Table of Contents

Chapter 8: The Future of NLP Transformers: Trends and Research Directions

8.1 Emerging Transformer Architectures and Advancements
8.2 Responsible NLP Development: Fairness, Safety, and Explainability
8.3 The Expanding Applications of NLP Transformers

Chapter 1
Introduction

The ever-growing field of Natural Language Processing (NLP) is revolutionizing how computers interact with human language. At the forefront of this progress lies the transformative power of NLP Transformers. These advanced machine learning models are pushing the boundaries of what's possible, enabling machines to understand and generate human language with unprecedented sophistication.

This comprehensive guide, Becoming Proficient in NLP Transformers, is designed to equip you with the knowledge and skills to navigate this exciting landscape. Whether you're a budding NLP enthusiast or an aspiring AI developer, this book will serve as your roadmap to mastering the art of NLP Transformers.

We'll embark on a journey that starts with the foundational concepts of NLP, ensuring you have a solid grasp of core tasks and text representation methods. Then, we'll delve into the captivating world of Transformers, demystifying their architecture and the ingenious attention mechanism that fuels their power.

Equipped with this knowledge, you'll be ready to dive into the practical aspects of building your first NLP Transformer model.

We'll explore the popular frameworks and libraries that empower development, guide you through data preparation and pre-processing techniques, and show you how to leverage the strengths of pre-trained transformers for your specific tasks.

The journey doesn't end there. We'll delve into the intricacies of training and optimizing your models, equipping you with the tools to achieve peak performance. You'll discover effective strategies to prevent overfitting, explore advanced techniques like transfer learning and multi-task learning, and gain insights into addressing challenges like bias and explainability in NLP Transformers.

Finally, we'll bridge the gap between theory and practice, guiding you through the process of deploying and utilizing your NLP Transformer model in real-world applications. We'll cover methods for saving and loading your trained models, explore integration with APIs and chatbots, and provide tips for ongoing monitoring and maintenance.

As we conclude, we'll set our sights on the horizon, exploring the exciting future of NLP Transformers and the cutting-edge research directions shaping the field. We'll discuss emerging architectures, the importance of responsible NLP development, and the ever-expanding applications of these transformative models.

This guide is more than just a collection of technical information; it's a springboard for your journey as an NLP Transformer expert. By the end, you'll be equipped with the knowledge, practical skills, and a thirst for further exploration to make your mark on the ever-evolving world of NLP.

So, are you ready to unlock the potential of NLP Transformers? Let's begin!

1.1 What are NLP Transformers?

NLP Transformers are a cutting-edge type of deep learning model that have revolutionized the field of Natural Language Processing (NLP). They excel at tasks that involve understanding the relationships between words in a sequence, making them particularly powerful for tasks like machine translation, text summarization, and question answering.

Here's a breakdown of what makes them special:

Attention Mechanism: At the core of a Transformer lies the attention mechanism. This ingenious approach allows the model to focus on specific parts of a sentence when processing it, rather than simply considering words in order. This enables them to capture long-range dependencies between words, a challenge faced by older NLP models.

Encoder-Decoder Architecture: Many Transformers follow an encoder-decoder architecture. The encoder takes an input sentence and creates a representation that captures its meaning. The decoder then uses this representation to generate an output, like a translated sentence or a summarized text.

State-of-the-art Performance: Due to their ability to capture complex relationships in language, Transformers have achieved state-of-the-art performance on a wide range of NLP tasks. They have become the go-to approach for many NLP applications.

In essence, NLP Transformers are like highly skilled language experts with an exceptional ability to understand the nuances and connections within human language. This makes them a powerful tool for unlocking the potential of machines to interact with and understand our world through the power of words.

1.2 Why are Transformers Important?

Here's why Transformers are important in the field of Natural Language Processing (NLP):

Breakthrough Performance: Transformers have achieved state-of-the-art results on a wide range of NLP tasks. They can outperform traditional models in areas like machine translation, text summarization, question answering, and sentiment analysis. This translates to real-world benefits like more accurate chatbots, improved document understanding for machines, and more natural-sounding machine-generated text.

Superior Long-Range Dependency Modeling: Unlike older NLP models that process text sequentially, Transformers excel at capturing long-range dependencies between words. This means they can understand how words far apart in a sentence relate to each other, crucial for tasks like translation and summarization where context is key.

Efficiency and Scalability: Transformers are known for their parallel processing capabilities. This allows them to analyze large amounts of text data simultaneously, leading to faster training and improved efficiency compared to traditional models. Additionally, they can handle sequences of varying lengths without sacrificing performance, making them adaptable to diverse NLP tasks.

Foundation for Future Advancements: The success of Transformers has paved the way for further innovation in NLP. Their architecture serves as a base for new research and development, pushing the boundaries of what's possible in language understanding and generation.

Unlocking Potential Applications: The high performance of Transformers opens doors to a vast array of potential applications. They can be used in everything from improving search engine results and generating realistic dialogue in chatbots to analyzing customer reviews and creating personalized educational experiences.

In essence, Transformers represent a significant leap forward in NLP capabilities. Their ability to understand complex language structures and achieve breakthrough performance makes them a crucial tool for unlocking the potential of machines to interact with and process human language effectively.

1.3 A Roadmap for This Guide

This comprehensive guide, Becoming Proficient in NLP Transformers, is designed to be your roadmap to mastering this revolutionary technology. We'll embark on a learning journey that progresses from foundational concepts to practical applications, equipping you with the knowledge and skills to confidently build and utilize your own NLP Transformers.

Here's a breakdown of the key stages we'll cover:

Foundations of NLP (Chapter 2): We'll establish a solid understanding of Natural Language Processing (NLP) by exploring core tasks like text classification and question answering. We'll delve into the concept of word embeddings, a crucial technique for representing text data numerically, which is essential for training machine learning models.

Demystifying Transformers (Chapter 3): Get ready to dive deep into the world of Transformers! We'll unveil their architecture, including the powerful encoder-decoder structure and the ingenious attention mechanism that lies at their heart. You'll gain insights into how these elements work together to enable Transformers to process and understand language with exceptional capability. We'll also explore some popular Transformer variations like BERT and GPT, giving you a broader perspective on this powerful technology.

Building Your First Model (Chapter 4): Now it's time to get hands-on! We'll guide you through the process of developing your first NLP Transformer model. This chapter will equip you with the knowledge to choose the right development framework (like TensorFlow or PyTorch) and leverage powerful libraries like Hugging Face Transformers. We'll cover essential data preparation and pre-processing techniques to ensure your model is trained on high-quality data. Finally, you'll learn how to fine-tune a pre-trained Transformer model for your specific NLP task, allowing you to harness the power of existing knowledge for your project.

Training and Optimization (Chapter 5): We'll delve into the world of training and optimizing your NLP Transformer model. This chapter will equip you with the tools to set up an effective training environment and explore various loss functions and evaluation metrics relevant to different NLP tasks. You'll discover techniques to prevent overfitting, a common challenge in machine learning, and learn how to fine-tune hyperparameters to achieve optimal performance from your model.

Advanced Techniques (Chapter 6): Ready to push the boundaries? This chapter explores advanced techniques that can elevate your NLP Transformer skills. We'll discuss transfer learning, a powerful approach that leverages knowledge from pre-trained models to enhance your own model's capabilities. You'll explore multi-task learning, a strategy for training a single model on multiple tasks simultaneously, leading to improved efficiency. We'll also address some of the challenges associated with NLP Transformers, such as bias and explainability, equipping you with the knowledge to develop responsible and ethical NLP models.

Deployment and Utilization (Chapter 7): The knowledge gained so far is valuable, but how do you put your NLP Transformer model to work in the real world? This chapter bridges the gap between theory and practice, guiding you through the process of saving and loading your trained models. We'll explore how to integrate your model into various applications, such as APIs and chatbots, allowing it to interact with users and perform real-world tasks. Finally, we'll provide tips for ongoing monitoring and maintaining your NLP Transformer model to ensure it continues to deliver optimal performance.

The Future of NLP Transformers (Chapter 8): As we approach the conclusion, let's set our sights on the horizon! This chapter explores the exciting future of NLP Transformers and the cutting-edge research directions shaping the field. We'll discuss emerging architectures that push the boundaries of performance and delve into the importance of responsible NLP development, ensuring these powerful models are used ethically and fairly. Finally, we'll explore the ever-expanding applications of NLP Transformers, highlighting the vast potential they hold for revolutionizing the way humans and machines interact with language.

This roadmap provides a glimpse into the exciting journey that awaits you within this guide. With dedication and a thirst for knowledge, you'll be well-equipped to unlock the transformative power of NLP Transformers and make your mark on this rapidly evolving field. So, are you ready to begin?

Chapter 2
Foundations of Natural Language Processing (NLP)

Before diving into the fascinating world of NLP Transformers, let's establish a solid foundation in Natural Language Processing (NLP) itself. This chapter will equip you with the essential concepts and techniques that underpin the development and application of NLP Transformers.

Here's what we'll explore:

Understanding Text Data: Natural language is complex and nuanced. This section will introduce you to the various ways computers represent and process textual data. We'll explore concepts like tokenization, where sentences are broken down into individual words, and stemming/lemmatization, which involves reducing words to their root form.

Core NLP Tasks: The field of NLP encompasses a wide range of tasks. We'll delve into some of the most fundamental ones, including:

Text Classification: Assigning categories or labels to text documents. For instance, classifying emails as spam or not spam.
Machine Translation: Automatically translating text from one language to another.

Question Answering: Extracting relevant answers to user queries from a given text corpus.

Text Summarization: Condensing lengthy pieces of text while preserving the key information.

Word Embeddings and Representing Text Numerically: Since computers don't understand language inherently, we need a way to convert text data into a numerical format they can process. This is where word embeddings come in. We'll explore techniques like Word2Vec and GloVe that learn vector representations of words, capturing semantic relationships between them. This numerical representation is crucial for training machine learning models to understand and manipulate language.

By understanding these foundational concepts, you'll gain a deeper appreciation for the challenges and opportunities that NLP Transformers address. This knowledge will serve as a springboard for effectively building and utilizing these powerful models in various NLP tasks.

2.1 Understanding Text Data

Natural language processing (NLP) revolves around a fundamental challenge: how to bridge the gap between the richness and complexity of human language and the structured, numerical world of computers. Text data, the raw material for NLP tasks, presents unique challenges due to its inherent ambiguity and variability.

This section will equip you with the foundational knowledge of how computers represent and process textual data, paving the way for a deeper understanding of how NLP Transformers work.

Challenges of Text Data:
Variability: Human language is full of variations. Words can have different spellings (e.g., "colour" vs. "color"), grammatical structures can differ, and slang or informal language can pose challenges for computers.

Ambiguity: Many words have multiple meanings depending on the context. For example, the word "bat" can refer to a flying mammal or a sporting equipment.
Non-linearity: Unlike numerical data, the order and relationships between words in a sentence are crucial for understanding its meaning.

Techniques for Representing Text Data:
To enable computers to analyze and process text data, we need to convert it into a format they can understand. Here are some key techniques:

Tokenization: The first step is to break down text into smaller units. This typically involves splitting sentences into individual words, but it can also involve further segmentation into smaller units like characters or n-grams (sequences of n consecutive words).

Normalization: Text data can be normalized in various ways to reduce its variability and improve processing efficiency. This may involve:

Lowercasing: Converting all letters to lowercase to eliminate case sensitivity.
Stemming: Reducing words to their base form (e.g., "running" becomes "run").

Lemmatization: Reducing words to their dictionary form (e.g., "running" becomes "run" and "better" becomes "good").
Word Embeddings: This is a crucial concept for NLP tasks. Word embeddings convert words into numerical vectors, capturing their semantic relationships and meaning within a specific context. Techniques like Word2Vec and GloVe learn these vector representations by analyzing large text corpora. This allows computers to process the relationships between words and understand the overall meaning of a sentence.

By understanding these techniques, you'll gain a deeper appreciation for the complexities of working with text data and the essential role these methods play in preparing text for NLP tasks like machine translation, text summarization, and – of course – building and utilizing NLP Transformers.

2.2 Core NLP Tasks: Text Classification, Machine Translation, Question Answering, etc.

The world of NLP encompasses a diverse range of tasks, each aiming to bridge the gap between human language and machine understanding. In this section, we'll delve into some of the most fundamental NLP tasks that NLP Transformers excel at:

1. Text Classification:

Description: This task involves automatically assigning categories or labels to text documents. Imagine sorting incoming emails into "spam" and "important" folders, or classifying product reviews as positive, negative, or neutral.

Applications: Text classification has a wide range of applications, including:

Sentiment analysis: Determining the overall positive, negative, or neutral sentiment expressed in a piece of text.
Spam filtering: Automatically identifying and filtering out spam emails.

Topic labeling: Categorizing news articles or social media posts based on their subject matter.

2. Machine Translation:

Description: This task involves automatically translating text from one language to another. Machine translation has become increasingly sophisticated, allowing for real-time communication across language barriers.

Applications: Machine translation powers a vast array of applications:

Real-time communication tools: Enabling conversations between people who speak different languages.
Multilingual content creation: Translating websites, documents, and marketing materials for a global audience.
Automated news translation: Allowing users to access news articles from around the world in their preferred language.

3. Question Answering (QA):

Description: This task focuses on extracting relevant answers to user queries from a given text corpus. Imagine a system that can answer your questions about a specific topic by searching through a vast collection of documents.

Applications: Question answering systems can be used in various ways:

Chatbots and virtual assistants: Providing users with information and completing tasks based on their questions.
Educational technology: Assisting students with their learning by answering questions about specific subjects.
Customer service: Offering automated support by answering frequently asked questions from customers.
.

4. Text Summarization:

Description: This task involves automatically generating a concise summary of a lengthy piece of text, capturing the key information while eliminating redundant details.

Applications: Text summarization can be beneficial in various scenarios:

News feeds: Providing users with quick summaries of news articles to help them stay informed.
Document analysis: Summarizing lengthy legal documents or research papers to improve comprehension.
Email overload: Generating summaries of lengthy email threads to help users stay on top of their inbox.

5. Other NLP Tasks:

Beyond these core tasks, NLP encompasses a wider range of functionalities, including:

Named Entity Recognition (NER): Identifying and classifying named entities in text, such as people, organizations, locations, and dates.
Part-of-Speech (POS) Tagging: Assigning grammatical tags to each word in a sentence (e.g., noun, verb, adjective).

Text Generation: Creating new text content, like poems, code, or scripts, based on a given set of prompts or instructions.

These tasks showcase the versatility of NLP and the potential of NLP Transformers to automate various language-related processes and unlock new avenues for human-computer interaction. As we delve deeper into this field, you'll gain insights into how Transformers address these tasks with exceptional efficiency and accuracy.

2.3 Word Embeddings and Representing Text Numerically

Bridging the gap between human language and the numerical world of computers is a fundamental challenge in NLP. Text data, rich with meaning and nuance, can't be directly processed by machines. This is where word embeddings come in – a powerful technique for converting words into numerical representations that computers can understand.

Here's why word embeddings are crucial for NLP tasks and how they pave the way for NLP Transformers:

The Challenge of Text Data:

Computers process information numerically. Text data, however, is full of complexities like ambiguity, synonymy (multiple words with similar meaning), and polysemy (words with multiple meanings depending on context).

The Power of Word Embeddings:

Word embeddings address these challenges by transforming words into numerical vectors. These vectors capture the semantic relationships between words, allowing computers to understand the meaning of a sentence based on the positions and interactions of the word vectors.

Popular Word Embedding Techniques:

Word2Vec: This technique analyzes large text corpora to learn vector representations of words. It considers the context in which words appear, capturing semantic relationships between them.

GloVe: Similar to Word2Vec, GloVe analyzes word co-occurrence statistics in a corpus to learn word vectors. It leverages statistical properties of word occurrences to create informative representations.

How Word Embeddings Benefit NLP Transformers:

Foundation for Machine Learning: By converting text data into numerical vectors, word embeddings provide the essential input format for training machine learning models like NLP Transformers.

Capturing Semantic Relationships: Word embeddings encode semantic similarities between words. This allows Transformers to understand the nuances of language and how words relate to each other within a sentence.

Enabling Efficient Processing: Numerical representations enable faster and more efficient processing of text data compared to traditional methods that work with raw text.

Examples of Word Embeddings in Action:

Imagine you have a sentence: "The quick brown fox jumps over the lazy dog."

Word embeddings would convert each word (the, quick, brown, etc.) into a numerical vector.

These vectors would capture the semantic relationships between the words. For instance, the vector for "quick" might be closer to the vector for "fast" than the vector for "lazy."

NLP Transformers, trained on massive amounts of text data with word embeddings, can then leverage these relationships to perform various NLP tasks. They can classify the sentiment of the sentence (positive), answer questions about the actions of the animals (the fox jumps), or even generate similar sentences with different vocabulary.

By understanding word embeddings, you gain a deeper appreciation for the foundation upon which NLP Transformers operate. These numerical representations unlock the potential for machines to process and understand the complexities of human language, paving the way for advancements in various NLP applications.

Chapter 3
Demystifying Transformers: Architecture and Mechanics

Now that you've grasped the fundamentals of NLP and the power of word embeddings, let's delve into the captivating world of Transformers! These innovative models have revolutionized NLP by excelling at tasks that involve understanding the relationships between words in a sequence. This section will unveil the inner workings of Transformers, demystifying their architecture and the ingenious mechanisms that fuel their success.

Unveiling the Transformer Architecture:
Encoder-Decoder Structure: Many Transformers follow an encoder-decoder architecture.

The encoder takes an input sentence and processes it word by word. It aims to capture the meaning and relationships within the sentence, converting it into a condensed representation.
The decoder utilizes the encoded representation generated by the encoder to produce an output, like a translated sentence, a summarized text, or an answer to a question.

Attention Mechanism: The Heart of Transformers: This is the revolutionary aspect of Transformers that sets them apart from traditional NLP models.

The attention mechanism allows the model to focus on specific parts of the input sentence when processing it, rather than simply considering words in order.
Imagine reading a sentence – you might pay more attention to certain words depending on the context. Similarly, the attention mechanism enables the Transformer to prioritize relevant parts of the sentence for understanding.

Benefits of the Attention Mechanism: By focusing on the most relevant parts of the input, the attention mechanism empowers Transformers to:

Understand long-range dependencies between words. This is crucial for tasks like machine translation, where the meaning of a sentence can depend on words that are far apart.
Capture the context of a word within a sentence. This allows for a more nuanced understanding of the overall meaning.
Process variable-length sequences more effectively. Unlike traditional models that struggle with sentences of different lengths, Transformers can handle them with ease.

Exploring Transformer Variations:

While the core architecture remains similar, there are various Transformer variations with specific strengths:

BERT (Bidirectional Encoder Representations from Transformers): A pre-trained Transformer model that excels at understanding the context of words in a sentence. It's widely used for tasks like question answering and text summarization.
GPT (Generative Pre-trained Transformer): Another pre-trained Transformer model, but with a focus on generating text. It can be used for tasks like creative text writing, dialogue generation, and machine translation.

By understanding these core concepts, you'll gain a solid foundation for appreciating the power and versatility of NLP Transformers. In the next chapters, we'll explore how to leverage these models for your own NLP tasks!

3.1 Encoder-Decoder Architecture

The encoder-decoder architecture is a fundamental concept underlying many NLP Transformers. It serves as a powerful approach for handling sequence-to-sequence tasks, where the model takes an input sequence (like a sentence) and generates an output sequence (like a translation or summary). Let's break down this architecture into its two key components:

1. The Encoder: Capturing Meaning from the Input Sequence

Imagine you're reading a book. The encoder acts like the part of your brain that processes each sentence and builds an understanding of the overall story. In the context of NLP Transformers:

The encoder takes an input sequence, typically a sentence represented as a series of word embeddings.

It processes each word embedding through multiple layers, using techniques like self-attention (explained later) to understand the relationships between words within the sentence.

With each layer, the encoder builds a more refined and contextualized representation of the input sequence.

By the end of the encoding process, the model has transformed the entire sentence into a condensed vector, capturing its core meaning and relationships.

2. The Decoder: Generating the Output Sequence

Now that you have a good grasp of the story from reading (thanks to the encoder), it's time to summarize it or translate it to another language. This is where the decoder comes in:

The decoder takes the encoded representation generated by the encoder as its starting point.

It also typically uses a special "start of sequence" token to initiate the generation process.

The decoder then employs another set of layers, often incorporating attention mechanisms (explained in the next section) to focus on relevant parts of the encoded representation as it generates the output sequence.

One word or element at a time, the decoder predicts the next item in the output sequence. This prediction can be another word in a translation task, a sentence in a summarization task, or something else depending on the specific application.

Benefits of the Encoder-Decoder Architecture:

Suitable for Sequence-to-Sequence Tasks: This architecture is specifically designed for tasks where the input and output are both sequences. It allows the model to effectively capture the meaning of the input sequence and translate it into a meaningful output sequence.

Flexibility for Diverse Tasks: By changing the decoder's output layer and training objectives, the encoder-decoder architecture can be adapted for various NLP tasks, including machine translation, text summarization, question answering, and more.

Modular Design: The separation of encoding and decoding allows for independent optimization of each component, potentially leading to better overall performance.

Understanding the encoder-decoder architecture is crucial for grasping how NLP Transformers process information and generate outputs. In the next section, we'll delve deeper into the magic behind their success – the attention mechanism.

3.2 Attention Mechanism: The Heart of Transformers

The attention mechanism is the revolutionary concept at the core of Transformers, setting them apart from traditional NLP models. It allows the model to focus on specific, relevant parts of the input sequence when processing it, rather than simply considering words in order. Imagine you're reading a sentence – you naturally pay closer attention to certain words depending on the context. Similarly, the attention mechanism empowers Transformers to prioritize informative parts of the sentence for a deeper understanding.

Here's a breakdown of how the attention mechanism works:

Calculating Attention Scores: For each word in the input sequence (represented by its word embedding), the attention mechanism calculates an attention score for every other word in the sequence. This score reflects how relevant each other word is to understanding the current word being processed.

Understanding the Math (Simplified): While the calculations involve matrices and vector operations, the core concept is relatively simple. The attention mechanism considers the compatibility between the current word's embedding and the embeddings of other words. Higher compatibility scores indicate a stronger relationship and a greater influence on understanding the current word.

Utilizing Attention Weights: Based on the calculated attention scores, the attention mechanism assigns attention weights to each word in the sequence. Words with higher scores receive higher weights, indicating their greater importance in understanding the current word.

Contextualized Representation: Finally, the attention mechanism creates a contextualized representation for the current word. This representation is a weighted sum of the embeddings of all the words in the sequence, where the weights are determined by the attention scores. In essence, the model focuses on the most relevant words when building a representation of the current word, taking context into account.

Benefits of the Attention Mechanism:

Capturing Long-Range Dependencies: Unlike traditional models that process words sequentially, the attention mechanism allows Transformers to understand how words far apart in a sentence relate to each other. This is crucial for tasks like machine translation, where word order can be significantly different between languages, and for tasks like question answering, where the answer might depend on keywords spread throughout the text passage.

Contextual Word Understanding: By focusing on relevant parts of the sentence, the attention mechanism allows Transformers to understand each word within its context. This leads to a more nuanced understanding of the overall meaning of the sentence.

Efficiency with Variable Length Sequences: Traditional models often struggle with sequences of varying lengths. The attention mechanism, however, allows Transformers to handle sequences of different lengths effectively, as the attention scores are calculated dynamically based on the specific input.

The attention mechanism is a powerful innovation that has revolutionized the field of NLP. By enabling Transformers to focus on relevant information and capture long-range dependencies, it unlocks a deeper understanding of language and empowers these models to excel at various NLP tasks. In the next chapter, we'll explore how to put this knowledge into practice by building your first NLP Transformer model!

3.3 Understanding Transformer Variations (e.g., BERT, GPT)

The core encoder-decoder architecture with the attention mechanism forms the foundation of many powerful Transformers. However, the NLP world boasts a rich tapestry of Transformer variations, each tailored for specific strengths and applications. This section will introduce you to two prominent examples: BERT and GPT, showcasing how they leverage the core Transformer architecture for distinct purposes.

1. BERT (Bidirectional Encoder Representations from Transformers):

Focus: Understanding Text and Context

Core Functionality: BERT is a pre-trained Transformer model, meaning it's trained on a massive dataset of text and text pairs (like sentences and their corresponding labels). This pre-training allows it to capture rich linguistic knowledge that can be applied to various downstream NLP tasks.

Architecture: Unlike the standard encoder-decoder structure, BERT utilizes only the encoder portion of the Transformer. It employs a masked language modeling technique where it randomly masks words in the input sentence and attempts to predict the masked words based on the surrounding context. This approach allows BERT to develop a deep understanding of how words relate to each other and their overall role within a sentence.

Applications: BERT excels at tasks that require comprehending the contextual nuances of language. Some of its common applications include:

Question Answering: BERT can analyze a passage of text and answer questions about its content by leveraging its contextual understanding.

Text Summarization: By understanding the key ideas and relationships within text, BERT can generate concise summaries that capture the essence of a document.
Sentiment Analysis: BERT can analyze the sentiment of text by considering the context of the words used and their relationships within the sentence.

2. GPT (Generative Pre-trained Transformer):

Focus: Text Generation

Core Functionality: Similar to BERT, GPT is also a pre-trained Transformer model. However, its training focuses on text generation. It's trained on a massive dataset of text where it predicts the next word in a sequence based on the preceding words. This approach allows GPT to learn the statistical patterns of language and generate human-quality text.

Architecture: GPT primarily utilizes the decoder portion of the Transformer architecture. During training, it receives a sequence of words as input and predicts the next word in the sequence. The attention mechanism plays a crucial role here, allowing GPT to focus on relevant preceding words to make informed predictions about the upcoming word.

Applications: GPT's strength lies in its ability to generate creative and coherent text formats. Some of its common applications include:

Creative Text Writing: GPT can be used to generate different creative text formats like poems, code, scripts, or musical pieces.
Dialogue Generation: GPT can be fine-tuned to generate realistic and engaging dialogue for chatbots or virtual assistants.
Machine Translation: While not its primary focus, GPT can be fine-tuned for machine translation tasks, leveraging its ability to generate sequences based on the preceding context.

Key Differences Between BERT and GPT:

https://docs.google.com/spreadsheets/d/1r_w2qpbKV_S8xsxOc
zfHLF1B9gpbKZcGuPhImMStOIY/edit?usp=drivesdk

Understanding these variations is crucial because choosing the right Transformer model for your NLP task depends on the specific goal. If your task involves understanding the meaning and relationships within text, BERT might be a strong choice. On the other hand, if your goal is to generate creative text formats or realistic dialogue, GPT could be more suitable.

As you delve deeper into the world of NLP Transformers, you'll encounter a wider range of variations, each with its own strengths and weaknesses. By understanding the core concepts behind BERT and GPT, you'll be well-equipped to navigate this ever-evolving landscape and choose the most appropriate Transformer model for your NLP endeavors.

Chapter 4

Developing Your First NLP Transformer Model

The world of NLP Transformers can seem complex, but with the right foundation and guidance, you can embark on your journey to building your first model. This section will equip you with a roadmap, breaking down the process into manageable steps:

1. Choosing Your Task and Dataset:

The first step is to identify the specific NLP task you want your Transformer model to perform. This could be something like text classification, sentiment analysis, question answering, or text summarization.

Once you've chosen your task, you'll need to find a suitable dataset. Many publicly available datasets cater to various NLP tasks. Popular platforms like Hugging Face Datasets (https://huggingface.co/docs/datasets/en/index) offer a rich collection of datasets with easy access through code.

2. Selecting a Pre-trained Transformer Model:

As discussed earlier, leveraging pre-trained Transformer models is a powerful approach. These models are already trained on massive amounts of text data, giving them a strong foundation for understanding language.

Popular choices for pre-trained Transformers include BERT and GPT, each with their strengths depending on your chosen task (refer to the previous section for their specializations).

3. Fine-tuning the Pre-trained Model:

While pre-trained models are powerful, they need to be fine-tuned for your specific task. This involves adapting the model's final layers to the specific requirements of your chosen NLP task and dataset.

4. Setting Up Your Development Environment:

You'll need to set up a development environment equipped with libraries like TensorFlow or PyTorch, commonly used for deep learning tasks. Additionally, libraries like Hugging Face Transformers (https://huggingface.co/docs/transformers/en/index) provide a user-friendly interface for working with pre-trained Transformers.

5. Preprocessing Your Text Data:

Text data needs to be preprocessed before feeding it into your model. This may involve tasks like tokenization (breaking down text into words), converting text to lowercase, and potentially stemming or lemmatization (reducing words to their root forms).

6. Training Your Model:

Once you have your pre-trained model, dataset, and preprocessed data ready, it's time to train your model! This involves feeding the data into the model and iteratively adjusting its internal parameters to minimize a loss function specific to your chosen NLP task.

7. Evaluating Your Model's Performance:

After training, you need to evaluate your model's performance. This typically involves setting aside a portion of your dataset for validation and testing. You can then measure metrics relevant to your task, such as accuracy for classification tasks or BLEU score for machine translation tasks.

8. Refining and Improving Your Model:

The journey doesn't end after training your first model. Machine learning is an iterative process. Analyze your evaluation results and identify areas for improvement. You can try different hyperparameter tuning techniques, explore variations of pre-trained models, or experiment with different preprocessing methods to potentially enhance your model's performance. Additional Resources:

Hugging Face Transformers Tutorial: https://huggingface.co/docs/transformers/en/index TensorFlow Tutorials: https://www.tensorflow.org/tutorials PyTorch Tutorials: https://pytorch.org/tutorials/

Developing your first NLP Transformer model can be an exciting and rewarding experience. By following these steps and leveraging the wealth of online resources available, you can step into the world of NLP Transformers and witness their power firsthand. Remember, this is just the beginning – as you gain experience, you can explore more advanced techniques and push the boundaries of what's possible in the realm of NLP!

4.1 Choosing a Framework (TensorFlow, PyTorch) and Libraries (Hugging Face Transformers)

When building your first NLP Transformer model, you'll need to make two key choices:

Deep Learning Framework: This is the foundation for building and training your model. Popular choices include TensorFlow and PyTorch.

NLP Library: This provides pre-trained Transformer models, helper functions, and optimizations specifically designed for NLP tasks. Hugging Face Transformers is a prominent library in this space.

Here's a breakdown to help you navigate these choices:

Deep Learning Frameworks:

TensorFlow: A mature and versatile framework from Google, offering a wide range of features and functionalities for deep learning tasks. It can be less user-friendly for beginners due to its lower-level API. However, TensorFlow offers extensive documentation and a large community for support.

PyTorch: A popular framework known for its dynamic computational graph and ease of use. Its Python-like syntax makes it more intuitive for beginners to grasp. PyTorch might be less scalable for exceptionally large models compared to TensorFlow.

Choosing Between TensorFlow and PyTorch:

There's no single "best" choice. Here are some factors to consider:

Your experience level: If you're new to deep learning, PyTorch's user-friendliness might be a plus.

Project requirements: Consider the scale and complexity of your NLP task. TensorFlow might be better suited for very large models.

Community and resources: Both frameworks have active communities and abundant resources. Explore tutorials and documentation for each to see which resonates more with you.

Hugging Face Transformers:

Regardless of the deep learning framework you choose, Hugging Face Transformers is a powerful library that simplifies working with pre-trained Transformers. It offers:

A repository of pre-trained Transformers: You can access a vast collection of pre-trained models like BERT, GPT, and others, all optimized for various NLP tasks.

Fine-tuning functionalities: Hugging Face Transformers provides tools to easily fine-tune pre-trained models for your specific NLP task and dataset.

Easy integration with TensorFlow and PyTorch: The library is compatible with both frameworks, allowing you to leverage the strengths of your chosen deep learning environment.

In summary:

Deep Learning Framework: Consider your experience level, project requirements, and personal preference when choosing between TensorFlow and PyTorch. Explore tutorials and resources for each to make an informed decision.

Hugging Face Transformers: This library is a valuable asset regardless of your deep learning framework choice. It streamlines working with pre-trained Transformers and empowers you to build effective NLP models.

Remember, the most important factor is to get started and begin your journey into the exciting world of NLP Transformers!

4.2 Data Preparation and Preprocessing for Transformers

Before unleashing the power of Transformers on your NLP task, you'll need to meticulously prepare your data. Just like any machine learning model, Transformers require clean, structured, and informative data to function effectively. This section will guide you through the essential steps of data preparation and preprocessing for training your Transformer model:

1. Data Acquisition:

The first step is to gather the data you'll use to train your Transformer model. This data can come from various sources, depending on your chosen NLP task:

Public Datasets: Many publicly available datasets cater to various NLP tasks. Popular platforms like Hugging Face Datasets (https://huggingface.co/docs/datasets/en/index) offer a rich collection with easy access through code.

Web Scraping: If you can't find a suitable public dataset, you can consider web scraping techniques to collect relevant text data from the web. Remember to adhere to ethical scraping practices and website terms of service.

Private Data Sources: You might have access to private data sources relevant to your specific NLP task. Ensure you have the necessary permissions and anonymize any sensitive information before using it for training.

2. Data Cleaning and Inspection:

Raw data often contains inconsistencies, errors, and irrelevant information. This step involves cleaning your data to ensure its quality:

Identify and remove duplicates: Eliminate redundant data points that might skew your model's training.

Handle missing values: Decide on a strategy to address missing values in your data, such as imputation techniques or removal.

Correct errors: Fix typos, grammatical mistakes, or any inconsistencies present in the text data.

3. Text Normalization:

Text data can vary significantly in terms of capitalization, punctuation, and spelling. Normalization helps create consistency:

Lowercasing: Convert all text to lowercase to eliminate case sensitivity.

Punctuation removal: Decide whether to remove punctuation marks entirely or keep essential ones for specific tasks (e.g., question marks for sentiment analysis).

Spelling normalization: Address common typos and misspellings to ensure consistency within your data.

4. Tokenization:

Transformers process text data sequentially, one unit at a time. Tokenization breaks down your text data into these smaller units:

Word Tokenization: The most common approach, where sentences are split into individual words.

Subword Tokenization: For languages like Chinese, which lack word delimiters, subword units (like characters or morphemes) might be used.

5. Text Encoding:

Computers don't understand text directly. We need to convert the tokens (words or subwords) into numerical representations:

Word Embeddings: Powerful techniques like Word2Vec or GloVe pre-train word embeddings that capture semantic relationships between words. These pre-trained embeddings can be loaded and used directly in your Transformer model.

Integer Encoding: Assigning a unique integer to each word in your vocabulary. This is a simpler approach but might not capture semantic relationships effectively.

6. Padding and Truncation:

Text data can have varying lengths. Transformers typically require sequences of a fixed length for processing:

Padding: Sequences shorter than the fixed length are padded with special tokens (e.g., padding tokens) to reach the required length.

Truncation: Sequences exceeding the fixed length are truncated, typically at the beginning or end of the sequence. Decide on a truncation strategy that minimizes information loss for your specific task.

7. Building the Vocabulary (Optional):

Depending on your chosen text encoding method (e.g., integer encoding), you might need to create a vocabulary that maps each unique word in your dataset to a unique integer. This vocabulary will be used for encoding new text data during inference.

Tools and Libraries for Data Preprocessing:

Hugging Face Transformers: This library provides helper functions for many of the preprocessing steps mentioned above, making it easier to work with text data for Transformers.

Regular Expressions: Libraries like re in Python can be helpful for tasks like text cleaning and normalization.

Natural Language Toolkit (NLTK): A popular toolkit offering functionalities for various NLP tasks, including text processing and tokenization.

By following these data preparation and preprocessing steps, you'll ensure your Transformer model receives clean, informative, and well-structured data, ultimately leading to better training performance and more accurate results for your NLP tasks. Remember, the specific preprocessing techniques you employ might vary depending on your chosen NLP task and the characteristics of your data.

4.3 Fine-tuning a Pre-trained Transformer Model for Your Task

The world of NLP Transformers offers a treasure trove of pre-trained models like BERT and GPT, already equipped with vast knowledge from training on massive text corpora. However, to unlock their true potential for your specific NLP task, you'll need to fine-tune them. This section delves into the concept of fine-tuning and how it empowers you to harness the strengths of pre-trained Transformers for your unique NLP endeavors.

Understanding Fine-tuning:

Imagine a master chef with a range of culinary skills. Fine-tuning a pre-trained Transformer is analogous to taking this master chef and teaching them the specifics of a new cuisine. Here's how it works:

Pre-trained Transformer as a Foundation: The pre-trained model serves as a powerful starting point, encapsulating valuable knowledge about language from its extensive training. This knowledge is stored in the model's weights and biases across its various layers.

Freezing the Early Layers: The initial layers of the pre-trained model typically capture foundational linguistic knowledge like recognizing patterns and understanding grammatical structures. These layers are often frozen during fine-tuning to preserve this valuable general knowledge.

Fine-tuning the Later Layers: The later layers of the pre-trained model are responsible for task-specific knowledge. During fine-tuning, these layers are retrained with your specific dataset and task in mind. This allows the model to adapt its understanding of language to the particular requirements of your NLP task.

Benefits of Fine-tuning:

Leveraging Pre-trained Knowledge: Fine-tuning allows you to benefit from the extensive knowledge already captured in the pre-trained model, reducing training time and effort compared to training a model from scratch.

Improved Performance: By adapting the model to your specific task, fine-tuning can significantly improve its performance on your NLP task.

Reduced Training Data Needs: Fine-tuning often requires less data compared to training a model from scratch. This is because the pre-trained model already has a strong foundation in understanding language.

Fine-tuning in Action (Example):

Imagine you're training a BERT model for sentiment analysis. Here's a simplified breakdown:

You load a pre-trained BERT model.

You freeze the initial layers of BERT that capture general linguistic knowledge.

You add a new layer or modify the final layers of BERT specific to sentiment analysis.

You train the model on your sentiment analysis dataset, fine-tuning the later layers to distinguish between positive, negative, and neutral sentiment.

Fine-tuning Techniques and Considerations:

Choosing the Right Pre-trained Model: Select a pre-trained model with strengths aligned with your NLP task. For sentiment analysis, BERT might be suitable, while GPT might be better for text generation tasks.

Data Augmentation Techniques (Optional): If your dataset is limited, consider data augmentation techniques to artificially expand your data and improve the fine-tuning process.

Hyperparameter Tuning: Experiment with different hyperparameters like learning rate and batch size to optimize the fine-tuning process for your model's performance.

Fine-tuning is a powerful technique that unlocks the true potential of pre-trained Transformers for your NLP tasks. By understanding the core concepts and following best practices, you can leverage these fine-tuned models to achieve impressive results in various NLP domains.

Chapter 5
Training and Optimizing NLP Transformers Effectively

Training NLP Transformers can be an exciting yet intricate process. To harness their full potential, careful consideration of training strategies and optimization techniques is crucial. This section equips you with valuable knowledge to train and optimize your NLP Transformer models effectively.

1. Setting Up Your Training Environment:

Deep Learning Framework: Choose a framework like TensorFlow or PyTorch that aligns with your preferences and project requirements (refer to the previous section on choosing a framework).
Hugging Face Transformers: Leverage this library for easy integration of pre-trained models, fine-tuning functionalities, and compatibility with your chosen deep learning framework.
Hardware Considerations: Training Transformers can be computationally expensive. Utilize GPUs or specialized hardware accelerators if available to expedite the training process.

2. Preparing Your Training Data:

Ensure your data is well-preprocessed following the steps outlined in the previous section on data preparation. This includes cleaning, normalization, tokenization, and encoding your text data.

Split your data into training, validation, and test sets. The training set is used to train the model, the validation set is used to monitor performance during training and adjust hyperparameters if needed, and the test set is used for final evaluation of the model'sgeneralizability after training is complete.

3. Defining the Training Loop:

The training loop is the core iterative process where your model learns from your data. Here's a simplified breakdown:

Forward Pass: The model takes an input batch of data, processes it through its layers, and generates predictions.

Loss Calculation: The model's predictions are compared to the actual labels in the training data to calculate a loss value, which quantifies the model's errors.

Backward Pass: The loss value is propagated back through the network, updating the weights and biases of the model's layers in a direction that minimizes the loss.

Optimization Step: An optimizer algorithm (like Adam or SGD) utilizes the calculated gradients to update the model's parameters.

4. Selecting an Optimizer:

The optimizer algorithm plays a critical role in guiding the training process. Popular choices include:

Adam: An adaptive learning rate optimizer that adjusts learning rates for each parameter based on historical gradients, often a good default choice.

SGD (Stochastic Gradient Descent): A simpler optimizer that updates parameters based on the gradients of a single data point or a small batch of data points.

5. Hyperparameter Tuning:

Hyperparameters control the learning process of your model. Examples include learning rate, batch size, and the number of training epochs. Finding the optimal hyperparameter configuration can significantly impact your model's performance. Techniques like grid search or random search can be used to explore different hyperparameter combinations and identify the configuration that yields the best results on your validation set.

6. Monitoring Training Progress:

Closely monitor your model's performance during training using metrics relevant to your NLP task. Common metrics include accuracy for classification tasks, F1-score for question answering, or BLEU score for machine translation. Track metrics on both the training and validation sets. Ideally, the training loss should decrease, and the validation metric should improve over time. Significant discrepancies between training and validation performance might indicate overfitting and the need for regularization techniques.

7. Regularization Techniques:

Regularization techniques help prevent overfitting, a situation where the model performs well on the training data but fails to generalize well to unseen data. Common approaches include:
Dropout: Randomly dropping neurons from the network during training, forcing the model to learn robust features that are not dependent on specific neurons.
L1/L2 Regularization: Penalizing the model for having large weights, encouraging the model to learn sparser representations and avoid overfitting.

8. Early Stopping:

Early stopping is a technique to prevent overfitting by stopping the training process when the validation metric stops improving. This helps to avoid the model from memorizing the training data and sacrificing its ability to generalize to new data.
By following these guidelines and carefully crafting your training process, you can effectively train and optimize your NLP Transformer models, unlocking their true potential for exceptional performance on your NLP tasks. Remember, training Transformers can be an iterative process. Experiment

with different techniques, monitor your results, and fine-tune your approach to achieve optimal outcomes.

5.1 Setting Up a Training Environment

The foundation for training NLP Transformers lies in establishing a well-configured development environment. Here's a breakdown of the essential components to get you started:

1. Hardware:

GPU Acceleration (Recommended): Training Transformers can be computationally intensive. Utilizing a Graphics Processing Unit (GPU) can significantly accelerate the training process compared to using a CPU alone. GPUs are particularly adept at handling the parallel computations involved in deep learning tasks. If budget or resource limitations prevent GPU access, training on a CPU is still possible, but expect longer training times.

RAM Considerations: The amount of RAM you'll need depends on the size and complexity of your chosen Transformer model and your dataset. A minimum of 16GB of RAM is recommended, with 32GB or more being ideal for larger models or datasets.

2. Software:

Deep Learning Framework: Choose a deep learning framework that serves as the foundation for building and training your model. Popular choices for NLP tasks include:

TensorFlow: A mature and versatile framework from Google, offering a wide range of features for deep learning. It can have a steeper learning curve for beginners.

PyTorch: A user-friendly framework known for its dynamic computational graph and ease of use. It might be less scalable for exceptionally large models compared to TensorFlow.

Hugging Face Transformers: Regardless of your chosen deep learning framework, this library is a valuable asset. It simplifies working with pre-trained Transformers by providing:

Access to Pre-trained Models: You can explore a vast collection of pre-trained models like BERT, GPT, and others, all optimized for various NLP tasks.

Fine-tuning Functionalities: Hugging Face Transformers offers tools to easily fine-tune pre-trained models for your specific NLP task and dataset.

Integration with TensorFlow and PyTorch: The library seamlessly integrates with both frameworks, allowing you to leverage the strengths of your chosen environment.

3. Package Installation:

Once you've decided on your deep learning framework, you can install it along with Hugging Face Transformers and other necessary libraries using a package manager like pip (for Python). Here's an example command for installing TensorFlow and Hugging Face Transformers:

```Bash
pip install tensorflow transformers
Use code with caution.
content_copy
```

4. Python Environment (Optional):

Consider creating a virtual environment using tools like venv or conda to isolate the dependencies for your project. This helps to manage project-specific libraries and avoid conflicts with other Python environments on your system.

..

5. Text Editor or IDE:

Choose a code editor or Integrated Development Environment (IDE) that suits your preferences for writing and debugging Python code. Popular options include Visual Studio Code, PyCharm, or Jupyter Notebook. Some IDEs offer features specifically tailored for deep learning tasks, which can enhance your development experience.

Additional Tips:

GPU Compatibility: Ensure your chosen deep learning framework is compatible with your GPU and that you have the necessary drivers installed. Consult the framework's documentation for specific instructions.

CUDA Toolkit (for NVIDIA GPUs): If you're using an NVIDIA GPU, you might need to install the CUDA Toolkit, which provides libraries for GPU programming.

Online Resources: Refer to the official documentation of your chosen deep learning framework and Hugging Face Transformers for detailed installation guides, tutorials, and troubleshooting resources.

By setting up a well-equipped training environment, you'll be ready to embark on your journey of training and fine-tuning NLP Transformer models for various tasks. Remember, the specific hardware and software requirements might vary depending on the complexity of your chosen model and dataset.

5.2 Loss Functions and Evaluation Metrics for NLP Tasks

When venturing into the world of NLP Transformers, understanding how to assess your model's performance is crucial. This section explores two key concepts: loss functions and evaluation metrics. These tools work hand-in-hand to guide your model's training and evaluate its effectiveness on NLP tasks.

1. Loss Functions: Steering the Training Process

Imagine you're training a model to navigate a maze. The loss function acts like a distance indicator, telling the model how far it is from the goal (correct prediction) on each training example. By minimizing this loss during training, the model iteratively adjusts its internal parameters to make better predictions. Here are some common loss functions used in NLP tasks:

Cross-Entropy Loss (Classification): A popular choice for classification tasks, where the model predicts a class label (e.g., positive or negative sentiment). The loss measures the difference between the model's predicted probability distribution and the true probability distribution of the correct class.

Mean Squared Error (Regression): Used for regression tasks, where the model predicts a continuous value (e.g., rating score).

The loss calculates the average squared difference between the predicted values and the actual values in the training data.

Masked Language Modeling Loss: Specific to pre-trained models like BERT, this loss function measures the model's ability to predict masked words in a sentence based on the surrounding context. This loss helps the model develop a strong understanding of language relationships.

2. Evaluation Metrics: Assessing Model Performance

The loss function guides the training process, but it doesn't tell the whole story. Evaluation metrics provide a broader picture of how well your model performs on unseen data after training is complete. Here are some common evaluation metrics used in NLP tasks:

Accuracy (Classification): The percentage of predictions that the model gets correct.

Precision and Recall (Classification): Precision measures the proportion of positive predictions that are truly correct, while recall measures the proportion of actual positive cases that the model correctly identifies.

F1-Score (Classification): A harmonic mean of precision and recall, combining both metrics into a single score.

BLEU Score (Machine Translation): Evaluates the quality of machine translation by comparing a generated translation to a set of reference translations. It considers factors like n-gram precision (matching sequences of words) to assess similarity.

Choosing the Right Metrics:

The choice of evaluation metric depends on the specific NLP task. Here are some general considerations:

Classification Tasks: Accuracy, F1-score, or metrics like precision and recall depending on the relative importance of avoiding false positives or false negatives.

Regression Tasks: Mean Squared Error (MSE) or other error metrics that quantify the difference between predicted and actual values.

Machine Translation Tasks: BLEU score or other metrics that evaluate the fluency and grammatical correctness of the generated translations.

Remember: Loss functions and evaluation metrics are complementary tools. The loss function guides training, while evaluation metrics assess the model'sgeneralizability on unseen data. By effectively utilizing both, you can ensure your NLP

Transformers are well-trained and perform exceptionally well on your chosen NLP tasks.

5.3 Regularization Techniques to Prevent Overfitting

.

Overfitting is a common challenge in machine learning, including training NLP Transformers. It occurs when a model memorizes the training data too closely, performing well on those specific examples but failing to generalize well to unseen data. Regularization techniques act as safeguards to prevent overfitting, allowing your NLP Transformer models to learn robust patterns and achieve better performance on unseen data. Here, we'll explore some common regularization techniques:

1. Dropout:

Imagine randomly dropping out some neurons (along with their connections) during training with a certain probability (e.g., 10% or 20%). This forces the model to learn from different subsets of neurons in each training iteration. The model cannot rely on any specific neuron and instead learns more robust features that are not dependent on a particular set of neurons. At test time, dropout is disabled, and all neurons are used for prediction.

2. L1 and L2 Regularization:

These techniques penalize the model for having large weights during training. Large weights can contribute to the model overfitting to the training data.

L1 Regularization (Lasso Regression): This technique introduces an L1 norm penalty term to the loss function. The L1 norm calculates the absolute sum of the weights. By minimizing the loss function with this penalty, the model is encouraged to drive many weights towards zero, effectively performing feature selection and promoting sparsity (having many weights equal to zero).

L2 Regularization (Ridge Regression): This technique uses an L2 norm penalty term in the loss function. The L2 norm calculates the sum of the squares of the weights. The penalty term discourages weights from becoming excessively large, leading to a smoother decision boundary and reducing overfitting.

3. Early Stopping:

This technique monitors the model's performance on a validation set during training. The validation set is a separate portion of your data not used for training. Early stopping halts the training process when the model's performance on the validation set starts to decline. This prevents the model from continuing to train on the training data and potentially overfitting to it.

Choosing the Right Regularization Technique:

The optimal choice of technique can depend on your specific task and dataset. Here are some general guidelines:

Dropout: A widely used and effective technique for various NLP tasks.

L1 Regularization: Consider L1 if you suspect some features might be irrelevant or if you want to perform feature selection during training.

L2 Regularization: A good general-purpose option, often used in conjunction with dropout.

Experimentation is key! Try different techniques and hyperparameter settings (e.g., dropout rate, L1/L2 penalty weights) to find the configuration that yields the best performance on your validation set and reduces overfitting.

Additional Tips:

Data Augmentation: If your dataset is limited, consider data augmentation techniques to artificially expand your data and improve the model'sgeneralizability.

Weight Decay: A specific technique that can be used with some optimizers (like Adam) to gradually decrease the weights of the model during training, implicitly introducing a form of L2 regularization.

By incorporating these regularization techniques into your training process, you can effectively prevent overfitting and train NLP Transformers that generalize well to unseen data, achieving superior performance on your NLP tasks.

5.4 5.4 Fine-tuning Hyperparameters for Optimal Performance

The success of your NLP Transformer hinges not only on the model architecture and training data, but also on a set of crucial dials known as hyperparameters. These parameters control the learning process itself, and fine-tuning them is an art form that can significantly impact your model's performance. This section delves into the world of hyperparameters and equips you with strategies for optimizing them for your NLP task.

Understanding Hyperparameters:

Imagine a master chef creating a dish. While the recipe (model architecture) and ingredients (data) are important, the success of the dish also depends on factors like cooking temperature and time (hyperparameters). These hyperparameters are not learned during training but are predetermined settings that influence how the model learns from the data. Examples of common hyperparameters in NLP Transformers include:

Learning Rate: This controls the step size the model takes when updating its weights during training. A high learning rate might lead to faster learning but can cause the model to jump past the optimal solution and potentially converge to a poor local minimum. Conversely, a very low learning rate might lead to slow training progress.

Batch Size: This determines the number of training examples used to update the model's weights in each iteration. A larger batch size can improve efficiency but might lead to the model overlooking subtle patterns in the data. Conversely, a smaller batch size can be more sensitive to noise but might require more training iterations.

Number of Training Epochs: This refers to the number of times the model iterates through the entire training dataset. Too few epochs might result in underfitting, where the model fails to learn the underlying patterns in the data. Conversely, too many epochs might lead to overfitting (discussed previously).

The Quest for Optimal Hyperparameters:

Unfortunately, there's no magic formula for finding the perfect hyperparameter configuration. It often involves experimentation and techniques like:

Grid Search: This method systematically evaluates a predefined grid of hyperparameter values. While comprehensive, it can be computationally expensive for a large number of hyperparameters.
..
Random Search: This approach randomly samples different hyperparameter combinations from a defined range. It can be more efficient than grid search for large search spaces and might be less likely to get stuck in local minima.
Bayesian Optimization: This advanced technique leverages past evaluations to prioritize promising hyperparameter combinations, making the search process more efficient.
Leveraging Libraries and Tools:

Hugging Face Transformers integrates well with deep learning frameworks like TensorFlow and PyTorch, offering functionalities to streamline hyperparameter tuning. Libraries like Optuna or Ray Tune can also be used for hyperparameter optimization tasks.

Key Considerations:

Start with Reasonable Defaults: Begin with common hyperparameter values used for similar NLP tasks as a baseline.

Track Performance Metrics: Closely monitor relevant evaluation metrics (accuracy, F1-score, etc.) on a validation set during hyperparameter tuning to assess the impact of different configurations.

Early Stopping During Tuning: Implement early stopping during hyperparameter evaluation to prevent excessive training time for poorly performing configurations.

Fine-tuning hyperparameters is an iterative process. By experimenting with different techniques, monitoring performance, and carefully considering your task and dataset, you can identify a hyperparameter configuration that unlocks the true potential of your NLP Transformer model.

Remember: The optimal hyperparameter configuration can depend on various factors, and there's no one-size-fits-all solution. The key is to experiment strategically and leverage available tools to find the settings that propel your NLP Transformer towards exceptional performance.

Chapter 6

Advanced Techniques for Pushing the Boundaries

Having explored the fundamentals of training and optimizing NLP Transformers, you might be eager to delve into more advanced territories. This section introduces some exciting techniques that can further enhance your models and push the boundaries of what's achievable in NLP tasks:

1. Multi-task Learning:

Train a single model on multiple NLP tasks simultaneously. This can be beneficial if the tasks share underlying representations or if you have limited labeled data for each individual task. For example, a model trained on sentiment analysis and question answering tasks might leverage shared knowledge about language understanding to improve performance on both tasks.

2. Transfer Learning with Large Language Models (LLMs):

Leverage the power of pre-trained LLMs like GPT-3 or Jurassic-1 Jumbo. These models are trained on massive datasets and can capture complex relationships within language. You can fine-tune an LLM on your specific NLP task, potentially achieving superior performance compared to fine-tuning smaller pre-trained models like BERT.

3. Ensemble Methods:

Combine multiple fine-tuned NLP Transformer models into an ensemble. By aggregating the predictions from different models, you can potentially achieve more robust and accurate results compared to a single model.

4. Prompt Engineering:

Craft effective prompts to guide the pre-trained model towards the desired task. Prompt engineering involves crafting specific natural language instructions or examples that prime the model to focus on the relevant aspects of the task. For example, instead of directly asking a model to write a poem, you could provide a prompt like "Write a poem in the style of William Wordsworth, about nature."

5. Utilizing Pre-training Objectives Beyond Masked Language Modeling:

Explore alternative pre-training objectives beyond Masked Language Modeling (MLM), which is a common technique used for pre-training models like BERT. Newer approaches like Replaced Token Detection (RTD) or Causal Language Modeling (CLM) might introduce different learning signals and potentially improve the model's capabilities on downstream NLP tasks.

6. Incorporating Domain-Specific Knowledge:

Integrate domain-specific knowledge into your model architecture or training process. This can involve using external knowledge graphs, leveraging task-specific embeddings, or incorporating domain-specific constraints during training. This can be particularly beneficial for tasks in specialized domains like healthcare or finance.

7. Exploring Hardware Advancements:

Keep an eye on advancements in hardware like specialized AI accelerators or TPUs (Tensor Processing Units) designed for deep learning tasks. Utilizing such hardware can significantly reduce training times for complex NLP Transformer models.

Remember: These advanced techniques often require more in-depth knowledge and experimentation. Start by mastering the fundamentals of training and optimizing NLP Transformers, and gradually progress towards incorporating these advanced approaches as you build your expertise.

The world of NLP Transformers is constantly evolving, and these techniques represent a glimpse into the exciting possibilities that lie ahead. By continuously learning, experimenting, and pushing the boundaries, you can be at the forefront of breakthroughs in NLP!

6.1 Transfer Learning with Pre-trained Transformers (BERT, XLNet, etc.)

The realm of NLP (Natural Language Processing) has been revolutionized by the emergence of pre-trained Transformer models like BERT and XLNet. These powerhouses, trained on vast amounts of text data, encapsulate valuable knowledge about language structure, semantics, and relationships between words. Transfer learning with these pre-trained models unlocks a powerful approach for tackling various NLP tasks, even with limited datasets. This section dives into the world of transfer learning with pre-trained Transformers.

The Core Idea of Transfer Learning:

Imagine a master chef with a vast culinary repertoire. Transfer learning treats this chef as a pre-trained model. When faced with a new cuisine (your NLP task), you don't need to train the chef from scratch (train a model from scratch). Instead, you leverage the chef's existing knowledge (pre-trained model's capabilities) and teach them the specifics of the new cuisine (fine-tune the model for your task). This significantly reduces training time and effort compared to building a model entirely from scratch.

Pre-trained Transformers: A Treasure Trove of Knowledge

Models like BERT and XLNet are pre-trained on massive datasets of text and code, allowing them to grasp intricate linguistic patterns and relationships between words. This knowledge is embedded within the model's weights and biases across its various layers. Here's a breakdown of the transfer learning process with pre-trained Transformers:

Load the Pre-trained Model: You start by loading a pre-trained Transformer model like BERT or XLNet, bringing its wealth of knowledge into your project.

Freeze the Early Layers (Optional): The initial layers of the pre-trained model capture foundational linguistic knowledge like recognizing patterns and understanding grammatical structures. These layers are often frozen during fine-tuning to preserve this valuable general knowledge.

Fine-tune the Later Layers: The later layers of the pre-trained model are responsible for more task-specific knowledge. During fine-tuning, these layers are retrained with your specific dataset and task in mind. This allows the model to adapt its understanding of language to the particular requirements of your NLP task.

Benefits of Transfer Learning with Pre-trained Transformers

Reduced Training Time and Resources: Leverage the pre-trained knowledge, significantly reducing the time and resources required to train a model from scratch.

Improved Performance: By adapting the model to your specific task, fine-tuning can lead to substantial performance improvements on your NLP task compared to training a model from scratch.

Reduced Data Requirements: Fine-tuning often requires less data compared to training a model from scratch because the pre-trained model already has a strong foundation in understanding language.

Examples of Transfer Learning Applications

Text Classification (Sentiment Analysis, Topic Classification): Fine-tune a pre-trained model to distinguish between positive, negative, and neutral sentiment in reviews, or classify documents according to different topics.

Question Answering: Train a model to answer questions by leveraging its understanding of language relationships and factual knowledge from the pre-trained model.

Machine Translation: Utilize a pre-trained model to translate text from one language to another, fine-tuning it for specific language pairs and domains.

Choosing the Right Pre-trained Model:

The choice of pre-trained model depends on your specific NLP task. Here are some considerations:

Task-Alignment: Select a model with strengths aligned with your task. For sentiment analysis, BERT might be suitable, while GPT-3 might be better for creative text generation tasks.

Model Size and Complexity: Consider the trade-off between model complexity (potentially higher accuracy) and training resource requirements.

Embrace the Power of Transfer Learning!

By leveraging pre-trained Transformers and transfer learning techniques, you can unlock remarkable performance gains in your NLP tasks. Remember, fine-tuning is an iterative process. Experiment with different models, hyperparameters, and techniques to achieve optimal results for your specific NLP endeavors. This approach empowers you to focus on the unique aspects of your task, while the pre-trained model handles the heavy lifting of understanding core language concepts.

6.2 Multi-task Learning for Enhanced Model Efficiency

In the realm of NLP (Natural Language Processing), training powerful models often requires significant computational resources and large datasets. Multi-task learning (MTL) emerges as a compelling approach to address this challenge, boosting model efficiency and unlocking its full potential with Transformers. This section explores how MTL leverages shared knowledge between related tasks, leading to improved performance and reduced training requirements.

The MTL Advantage: Learning from Multiple Tasks Simultaneously

Imagine training a single student (your NLP model) on multiple subjects (your NLP tasks) like grammar and literature. MTL allows the student to learn interconnected concepts, where knowledge from one subject (task) reinforces understanding in another. In NLP, MTL trains a single Transformer model on multiple related tasks concurrently. This approach offers several advantages:

Shared Representations: NLP tasks often share underlying linguistic concepts. MTL encourages the model to learn a single set of representations that can be effectively applied to multiple tasks. This reduces the model's overall complexity and training time compared to training separate models for each task.

Improved Data Efficiency: If labeled data is limited for a specific task, MTL can leverage knowledge from datasets of related tasks. The model can learn generalizable features that benefit all tasks, potentially mitigating the need for excessively large datasets for each individual task.

Enhanced Performance: By fostering the transfer of knowledge between tasks, MTL can lead to performance improvements on all tasks, especially when the tasks share significant similarities.

When Does MTL Shine?

MTL is particularly effective when dealing with NLP tasks that share underlying linguistic structures or require similar reasoning processes. Here are some prominent examples:

Sentiment Analysis and Text Classification: A model trained on both tasks can leverage shared knowledge about sentiment lexicons and textual patterns to improve performance on both tasks.

Question Answering and Natural Language Inference: Understanding relationships between words and concepts is crucial for both tasks. MTL can facilitate this process, leading to improved performance.

Machine Translation and Text Summarization: Both tasks involve understanding the meaning and structure of text. MTL can enhance the model's ability to perform both tasks effectively.

Implementing MTL with Transformers

There are various ways to implement MTL with Transformers. Here's a simplified approach:

Define Your Tasks: Identify the related NLP tasks you want the model to learn simultaneously.

Prepare Your Data: Ensure your datasets for each task are well-preprocessed and formatted for training.

Modify the Transformer Architecture: Depending on the chosen MTL approach, you might add additional task-specific layers on top of the shared representation layers of the pre-trained Transformer.

Design a Multi-task Loss Function: This function combines the loss signals from each individual task, guiding the model's learning process to optimize performance on all tasks collectively.

Challenges and Considerations in MTL

Task Difficulty Imbalance: Training performance can suffer if there's a significant discrepancy in the difficulty of the tasks. Consider techniques like weighted loss functions to address this issue.

Negative Transfer: In some cases, knowledge transfer between tasks can be negative, hindering performance on one or more tasks. Carefully selecting related tasks and monitoring performance during training is crucial.

MTL offers a powerful strategy to leverage the capabilities of Transformers for NLP tasks. By effectively sharing knowledge between related tasks, you can achieve significant gains in model efficiency and performance. Remember, experimentation with different MTL techniques and careful task selection are key to unlocking the full potential of this approach.

6.3 Addressing Challenges in NLP Transformers (Bias, Explainability

NLP Transformers, while powerful, are not without their challenges. As with any complex machine learning model, bias, explainability, and fairness can emerge as roadblocks on the path to achieving robust and ethical NLP applications. This section explores these challenges and offers strategies to mitigate them, ensuring your Transformers operate responsibly and transparently.

1. Bias: Unveiling and Mitigating Hidden Prejudices

NLP Transformers can inherit biases from the data they are trained on. Biased data can lead the model to make unfair or discriminatory predictions. Here are some ways to address bias:

Data Cleaning and Augmentation: Identify and remove biased examples from your training data. Consider data augmentation techniques to introduce more diversity and balance into your dataset.

Debiasing Techniques: Explore techniques like adversarial debiasing, which involves training a second model to identify and remove bias from the predictions of the main model.

Fairness Metrics: Monitor fairness metrics like F1 score disparity across different demographic groups to identify potential bias issues.

2. Explainability: Demystifying the Transformer's Decisions

Understanding how a Transformer model arrives at its predictions can be challenging. A lack of explainability can hinder trust and limit debugging capabilities. Here are some approaches to enhance explainability:

Attention Visualization Techniques: Tools can visualize which parts of the input text the model pays attention to when making a prediction, offering insights into the decision-making process.

Feature Importance Analysis: Identify the features or input elements that contribute most significantly to the model's predictions.

Explainable AI (XAI) Techniques: Utilize techniques like LIME (Local Interpretable Model-Agnostic Explanations) to create post-hoc explanations for individual model predictions.

3. Fairness: Ensuring Equitable Treatment for All

NLP Transformers should strive to treat all users fairly, regardless of background or characteristics. Here's how to promote fairness:

Balanced Datasets: Ensure your training data represents the diversity of the populations your model will be used on.

Fairness-aware Model Architectures: Explore architectures designed specifically to mitigate bias, such as incorporating fairness constraints during training.

Algorithmic Auditing: Regularly audit your model's performance across different subgroups to identify and address potential fairness issues.

The Road to Responsible NLP

Addressing bias, explainability, and fairness challenges is an ongoing endeavor. Here are some additional tips:

Transparency: Be transparent about the limitations of your model and the potential for bias.
Human oversight: Incorporate human review processes for critical decisions made by the model.

Collaboration: Engage with researchers and experts working on these challenges to stay informed and contribute to advancements in responsible NLP.

By actively confronting these challenges, we can ensure NLP Transformers become powerful tools that operate ethically and fairly, benefiting all users. Remember, responsible development and deployment are crucial for building trust and unlocking the full potential of NLP Transformers for positive impact in various domains.

Chapter 7
Deploying and Utilizing Your NLP Transformer Model in Practice

Once you've trained and fine-tuned your NLP Transformer model, it's time to unleash its potential! This section delves into the practical aspects of deploying your model and putting it to use in real-world scenarios.

Deployment Strategies:

Serving Frameworks: Frameworks like TensorFlow Serving, PyTorch Serving, or Flask can package your model for efficient serving. These frameworks handle model loading, input formatting, prediction generation, and output formatting, allowing you to focus on integrating the model into your application.

Cloud Platforms: Cloud platforms like Google Cloud AI Platform, Amazon SageMaker, or Microsoft Azure Machine Learning offer managed services for deploying and scaling NLP models. These services handle infrastructure management, scaling, and integration with other cloud services.

Containerization: Containerization technologies like Docker can package your model and its dependencies into a lightweight container. This simplifies deployment across different environments and ensures consistent behavior.

Considerations for Deployment:

Hardware Resources: The hardware resources required for deployment depend on your model's complexity and expected traffic. Consider factors like CPU, memory, and GPU availability when choosing a deployment environment.

Latency Requirements: For real-time applications, latency (response time) is crucial. Choose a deployment strategy that minimizes the time it takes for the model to generate predictions.

Scalability: If you anticipate high volumes of requests, ensure your deployment approach can scale to handle increased traffic. Cloud platforms or containerization can be beneficial for scalability.

Utilizing Your Deployed Model:

API Integration: Create a well-documented API (Application Programming Interface) that allows other applications to interact with your deployed model. This API should define the expected input format, output format, and any authentication requirements.

Client Applications: Develop client applications that leverage your model's API to perform NLP tasks. These applications can be web applications, mobile apps, or command-line tools tailored to your specific use case.

Monitoring and Feedback Loop: Continuously monitor your deployed model's performance in production. Track metrics like accuracy, latency, and error rates. Implement feedback loops to retrain the model with new data if performance degrades over time.

Best Practices:

Version Control: Maintain proper version control for your model code and deployment scripts. This allows you to track changes, revert to previous versions if necessary, and manage deployments efficiently.

Security: Secure your deployed model API with authentication and authorization mechanisms to prevent unauthorized access and potential misuse.

Documentation: Provide clear documentation for your deployed model, including the API specification, usage examples, and performance characteristics. This aids others in integrating and utilizing your model effectively.

By following these guidelines, you can successfully deploy your NLP Transformer model and unlock its capabilities in various real-world applications

. Remember, deployment is an ongoing process. Continuously monitor, improve, and adapt your model to ensure it delivers optimal performance and value over time.

7.1 Saving and Loading Trained Models

The journey of training an NLP Transformer model is a significant investment of time and resources. Once you've achieved a satisfactory level of performance, it's crucial to save your trained model for future use. This section explores techniques for saving and loading NLP Transformer models, allowing you to seamlessly resume work or deploy your model for real-world applications.

Popular Saving Formats for NLP Transformers:

TensorFlow SavedModel (.pb): A common format for TensorFlow models, suitable for both TensorFlow eager execution and TensorFlow Serving for deployment. It encapsulates the model architecture, weights, and optimizer state.

PyTorch SavedModel (.pt): The standard format for saving PyTorch models. It preserves the model's architecture, weights, and optimizer state.

ONNX (Open Neural Network Exchange): An open-source format for representing deep learning models. While not all Transformer functionalities might be directly convertible to ONNX, it offers portability across different deep learning frameworks.

Saving Your Trained Model:

Here's a general outline of the saving process, which can vary slightly depending on the chosen framework:

Import necessary libraries: Import the relevant libraries from TensorFlow, PyTorch, or a chosen serialization library.

Specify the model and optimizer: Identify the model object and optimizer instance you want to save.

Define the save path: Determine the file path where you want to store the saved model.

Utilize the saving function: Use the framework's built-in saving function (e.g., model.save() in TensorFlow or torch.save() in

PyTorch) to save the model and optimizer state to the specified location.

Loading a Saved Model:

When you're ready to resume training, evaluate, or deploy your model, you can load it from the saved files. The loading process generally mirrors the saving process:

Import necessary libraries: Import the relevant libraries for loading models.

Specify the model path: Provide the file path from where you want to load the saved model.

Use the loading function: Utilize the framework's model loading function (e.g., tf.keras.models.load_model() in TensorFlow or torch.load() in PyTorch) to load the model architecture, weights, and optimizer state from the specified location.

Additional Considerations:

Compatibility: Ensure compatibility between the framework versions used for saving and loading the model.

Custom Objects: If your model uses custom objects or functions, you might need to register them during loading to ensure proper functionality.

Partial Loading: Some frameworks allow you to selectively load specific parts of the model, such as only the weights, for certain use cases.

Beyond Saving the Model:

In addition to the model itself, consider saving other relevant information alongside it:

Training configuration: Save the training hyperparameters used (e.g., learning rate, batch size) to replicate the training process if needed.

Preprocessing steps: Document or save any preprocessing steps applied to the data during training to ensure consistent data handling when loading the model.

Evaluation metrics: Record the evaluation metrics (e.g., accuracy, F1-score) achieved during training to track the model's performance over time.

By effectively saving and loading your trained NLP Transformer models, you can streamline your development workflow, facilitate collaboration, and ensure the longevity of your valuable machine learning assets. Remember, clear documentation and proper version control practices complement these techniques, allowing you to manage your models effectively over time.

7.2 Integrating Your Model into Applications (APIs, Chatbots)

This section dives into integrating your model into various applications, transforming it from a standalone tool to a valuable component within a larger system. Here, we'll focus on two popular integration methods: APIs (Application Programming Interfaces) and chatbots.

API Integration:

An API acts as an intermediary, allowing other applications to interact with your NLP model without needing direct access to its inner workings. Here's how to approach API integration:

Choose a Framework: Select a framework like Flask or FastAPI (Python) or Express.js (JavaScript) to build your API. These frameworks provide tools for handling requests, responses, and data serialization.

Model Loading: Within your API code, load your trained NLP Transformer model using the appropriate techniques (covered in the "Saving and Loading Trained Models" section).

Define Input and Output Formats: Determine the format for data your API will accept (e.g., text strings, JSON objects) and the format of the response generated by your model (e.g., predicted labels, sentiment scores).

Develop API Endpoints: Create API endpoints that correspond to specific tasks your model can perform. For example, an endpoint for sentiment analysis might accept a text string as input and return a sentiment label (positive, negative, neutral).

Testing and Deployment: Thoroughly test your API to ensure it functions correctly and handles various input scenarios. Deploy your API to a cloud platform or a server to make it accessible to other applications.

Benefits of API Integration:

Modular Design: APIs promote modularity, allowing your model to be integrated into different applications without modification.

Scalability: APIs can handle multiple requests concurrently, facilitating scalability as your application usage grows.

Accessibility: APIs provide a standardized way for other developers to interact with your model, fostering wider adoption and collaboration.

Chatbot Integration:

Chatbots are interactive applications that simulate conversation with users. Integrating your NLP model into a chatbot empowers it to understand and respond to user queries in a more meaningful way. Here's a basic approach:

Develop Core Chatbot Functionality: Build the core functionalities of your chatbot, including handling user input, managing conversation flow, and generating responses.

NLP Model Integration: At appropriate points in the conversation flow, integrate your NLP model. For instance, you might use sentiment analysis to understand user emotions or employ a question-answering model to address user inquiries.

Response Generation: Based on the model's output and the conversation context, generate appropriate responses for the chatbot. This might involve leveraging natural language generation techniques or retrieving pre-defined responses based on the model's prediction.

Training and Improvement: Continuously train and improve your chatbot based on user interactions. Analyze user feedback and iteratively enhance your model's capabilities to provide more natural and informative conversations.

Advantages of Chatbot Integration:

Enhanced User Experience: NLP models empower chatbots to understand user intent and provide more relevant and engaging responses.

24/7 Availability: Chatbots can handle user interactions continuously, offering increased accessibility compared to human support agents.

Data Collection: Chatbot interactions can provide valuable data for further training and improvement of your NLP model.

Remember:

Security Considerations: Implement security measures like authentication and authorization to protect your API and chatbot from unauthorized access.

Error Handling: Design robust error handling mechanisms to gracefully handle unexpected inputs or model errors within your API or chatbot.

Monitoring and Analytics: Continuously monitor the performance of your API or chatbot. Utilize analytics tools to track user interactions and identify areas for improvement.

By effectively integrating your NLP Transformer model into APIs and chatbots, you can unlock its potential to transform user experiences and create intelligent interactive applications in various domains.

7.3 Monitoring and Maintaining Your NLP Transformer Model

Just like any complex system, NLP Transformer models require ongoing monitoring and maintenance to ensure optimal performance over time. This section delves into strategies for keeping your model healthy and performing at its best.

The Importance of Monitoring:

Imagine a car – you wouldn't drive it endlessly without checking the oil or tire pressure. Similarly, monitoring your NLP Transformer model is crucial for identifying potential issues and maintaining its effectiveness. Here's why monitoring is important:

Performance Degradation: Over time, a model's performance might degrade due to factors like data distribution shifts or concept drift (changes in the underlying concepts the model represents). Monitoring helps detect such issues early on.

Data Quality Issues: New data used for predictions might contain errors or deviations from the training data distribution. Monitoring can uncover these discrepancies to ensure the model generalizes well to unseen data.

Concept Drift: The real world is constantly evolving, and the language people use can change as well. Monitoring helps identify if the model's understanding of language needs to be updated with new data.

Key Metrics to Monitor:

Accuracy, Precision, Recall, F1 Score: These metrics evaluate how well your model classifies data points or makes predictions.

Latency: For real-time applications, monitor the time it takes for the model to generate predictions. High latency can hinder user experience.

Error Rates: Track the number of errors the model makes on different data subsets to identify potential biases or areas for improvement.

Monitoring Techniques:

Logging and Alerting: Set up a system to log model performance metrics and trigger alerts if they deviate significantly from expected values.

Data Drift Detection: Utilize techniques like statistical analysis or specialized libraries to detect shifts in the data distribution compared to the training data.

Human Evaluation: Regularly conduct human evaluation of the model's outputs to identify qualitative issues like nonsensical predictions or biased language usage.

Maintaining Your NLP Model:

Retraining: Based on monitoring results, you might need to retrain the model with new data that reflects the latest trends or addresses identified issues.

Fine-tuning: If the data distribution hasn't shifted significantly, fine-tuning the model with a small amount of new data can often improve performance.

Bias Monitoring: Continuously monitor for bias creep, especially if your model is used in sensitive applications. Consider techniques like fairness metrics and fairness-aware training methods.

Additional Tips:

Version Control: Maintain proper version control for your model code and training data. This allows you to revert to previous versions if necessary and track changes over time.

Documentation: Document your monitoring and maintenance procedures to ensure consistency and facilitate collaboration.

Stay Updated: The field of NLP Transformers is constantly evolving. Stay informed about new monitoring techniques, performance metrics, and best practices to keep your model on the cutting edge.

By implementing a proactive monitoring and maintenance strategy, you can guarantee that your NLP Transformer model continues to deliver reliable performance and adapts to the ever-changing world of language. Remember, effective monitoring is an ongoing process, and consistent attention is key to keeping your NLP Transformer model sharp and valuable over time.

Chapter 8
The Future of NLP Transformers: Trends and Research
Directions

The realm of NLP Transformers is constantly buzzing with innovation. As we peer into the future, exciting trends and research directions promise to revolutionize how we interact with language and push the boundaries of what's possible. Here, we'll explore some of the most promising advancements shaping the future of NLP Transformers:

1. Lifelong Learning for Transformers:

Current models often require significant retraining when faced with new data or evolving language patterns. Lifelong learning approaches aim to enable models to continuously learn and adapt throughout their deployment lifecycle, reducing the need for frequent retraining and improving real-world applicability.

Techniques like continual learning and online learning are being explored to facilitate this process. These methods allow the model to gradually incorporate new information without forgetting previously learned knowledge.

2. Enhanced Explainability and Interpretability:

The inner workings of complex NLP Transformers can be opaque, hindering trust and limiting debugging capabilities. The future holds promise for more explainable and interpretable models.

Research in this area delves into techniques like attention visualization and LIME (Local Interpretable Model-Agnostic Explanations) to provide insights into how the model arrives at its predictions. This will facilitate debugging, error analysis, and broader trust in model outputs.

3. Transformers for Multimodal Learning:

Language doesn't exist in isolation. The future envisions NLP Transformers seamlessly integrating with other modalities like vision and audio. This will allow models to process and understand information from various sources, leading to more robust and nuanced language comprehension.

Techniques like incorporating pre-trained image recognition models or learning joint representations for text and audio data are being explored to facilitate this fusion of modalities. This paves the way for applications like generating captions from images or summarizing video content.

4. Democratization of NLP Transformers:

Currently, training and deploying large NLP Transformers can require significant computational resources and expertise. The future forecasts a democratization of NLP Transformers, making them more accessible to a wider range of users.

Developments in areas like model compression, efficient training algorithms, and cloud-based solutions aim to reduce the computational burden associated with NLP Transformers. This will empower more individuals and organizations to leverage the power of these models.

5. Transformers for Human-like Reasoning and Dialogue Systems:

NLP Transformers are gradually evolving beyond mere pattern recognition and classification tasks. The future envisions models capable of reasoning, understanding context, and engaging in meaningful dialogue like humans.

Research in areas like commonsense reasoning and incorporation of external knowledge bases is underway. This paves the way for intelligent chatbots that can hold nuanced conversations, answer complex questions, and assist users in various tasks.

The Road Ahead

These are just a few glimpses into the exciting future of NLP Transformers. As research continues, we can expect even more groundbreaking advancements that will transform the way we interact with machines and understand the world around us. Staying informed about these emerging trends and research directions will be crucial for anyone wishing to remain at the forefront of NLP advancements.

Remember, the future of NLP Transformers is not predetermined. Our research choices and ethical considerations will shape how these powerful models are developed and deployed. By prioritizing responsible development and ensuring these advancements benefit society as a whole, we can unlock the true potential of NLP Transformers and create a brighter future for human-computer interaction.

8.1 Emerging Transformer Architectures and Advancements

The Transformer revolutionized natural language processing (NLP), achieving state-of-the-art performance on various tasks. However, researchers are continuously refining and expanding Transformer architectures to address limitations and unlock new capabilities. This section delves into emerging Transformer architectures and advancements that are shaping the future of NLP.

1. Efficient Transformers:

Standard Transformers can be computationally expensive to train and deploy, especially for large models. Efficient Transformer architectures focus on reducing computational complexity while maintaining performance.

Techniques like sparse attention mechanisms, reduced precision training, and knowledge distillation are being explored. Sparse attention methods focus the model's attention on a smaller subset of relevant elements, leading to significant computational savings. Reduced precision training utilizes lower-precision data types during training, allowing for faster training and smaller model footprints. Knowledge distillation involves training a smaller, more efficient model by transferring knowledge from a larger, pre-trained model.

2. Transformers for Long Sequences:

Standard Transformers struggle with long sequences due to vanishing gradients during training. Emerging architectures address this challenge by incorporating mechanisms that effectively capture long-range dependencies within sequences.

Techniques like recurrent layers within the Transformer architecture, dilated convolutions, and hierarchical Transformers are being explored. Recurrent layers allow the model to maintain information across longer sequences. Dilated convolutions capture dependencies between distant elements without increasing the receptive field exponentially. Hierarchical Transformers process sequences at different granularities, capturing both local and global dependencies.

3. Transformers with External Knowledge Integration:

While Transformers excel at learning from data, they often lack explicit knowledge about the world. Emerging architectures explore integrating external knowledge sources to enhance model capabilities.

Techniques like incorporating knowledge graphs or memory modules are being developed. Knowledge graphs encode factual information about entities and relationships, while memory modules allow the model to store and retrieve relevant information during processing. This integration facilitates reasoning and commonsense understanding.

4. Transformers for Generative Tasks:

Transformers have demonstrably powerful generative capabilities. Research is ongoing to refine these capabilities for various generative tasks like text summarization, dialogue generation, and machine translation.

Techniques like incorporating pointer-generator networks or adversarial training are being explored. Pointer-generator networks allow the model to flexibly generate text by either copying from the input sequence or creating new words. Adversarial training pits two models against each other, with one generating text and the other discriminating between real and generated text. This adversarial process encourages the generative model to produce more realistic and coherent outputs.

5. Pre-training Objectives for Transformers:

Pre-training on large text corpora plays a crucial role in the success of Transformers. Research is ongoing to develop more effective pre-training objectives that improve the model's ability to transfer learned knowledge to downstream tasks.

Techniques like masked language modeling, replaced token detection, and continual pre-training are being explored. Masked language modeling obscures a subset of words in the input and trains the model to predict them, fostering general contextual understanding. Replaced token detection trains the model to identify and correct replaced words, enhancing its ability to handle variations in language usage. Continual pre-training involves iteratively pre-training the model on new data and tasks, gradually refining its generalizability.

The Ever-Evolving Landscape

These advancements represent just a snapshot of the vibrant research landscape surrounding Transformer architectures. As research progresses, we can expect even more innovative architectures and techniques to emerge, pushing the boundaries of NLP and unlocking remarkable new applications for language processing.

Remember, the choice of Transformer architecture and advancements depends on the specific NLP task at hand. Carefully considering the task's requirements and available resources will guide you towards the most effective approach for your NLP project.

8.2 Responsible NLP Development: Fairness, Safety, and Explainability

.

As NLP Transformers become increasingly powerful, it's crucial to prioritize responsible development. This encompasses fairness, safety, and explainability to ensure NLP models operate ethically and avoid unintended consequences.

1. Fairness in NLP:

NLP models can inherit and amplify biases present in the data they are trained on. Biased models can make discriminatory predictions that disadvantage certain groups.

Techniques to Mitigate Bias:

Balanced Datasets: Ensure your training data represents the diversity of the populations your model will be used on.
Debiasing Techniques: Explore techniques like adversarial debiasing to remove bias from the model's predictions.
Fairness Metrics: Monitor fairness metrics like F1 score disparity across different demographic groups to identify potential bias issues.

2. Safety in NLP:

NLP models can be vulnerable to adversarial attacks where malicious actors intentionally craft inputs to mislead the model. Safety measures are essential to prevent such attacks and ensure the model produces reliable outputs.

Techniques to Enhance Safety:

Adversarial Training: Expose the model to adversarial examples during training to improve its robustness against such attacks.

Input Validation: Implement robust input validation mechanisms to detect and reject nonsensical or malicious inputs.

Human Oversight: Incorporate human review processes for critical decisions made by the model.

3. Explainability in NLP:

The inner workings of complex NLP models can be opaque, hindering trust and limiting debugging capabilities. Explainability techniques help us understand how the model arrives at its predictions.

Techniques to Improve Explainability:

Attention Visualization: Visualize which parts of the input text the model pays attention to when making a prediction.

Feature Importance Analysis: Identify the features or input elements that contribute most significantly to the model's predictions.

Explainable AI (XAI) Techniques: Utilize techniques like LIME (Local Interpretable Model-Agnostic Explanations) to create post-hoc explanations for individual model predictions.

The Importance of Responsible Development

Responsible development is not just a checkbox exercise. It's an ongoing commitment to ensure NLP models are beneficial to society. Here are some additional considerations:

Transparency: Be transparent about the limitations of your model and the potential for bias.

Collaboration: Engage with researchers and experts working on these challenges to stay informed and contribute to advancements in responsible NLP.

Data Privacy: Adhere to data privacy regulations and protect user privacy when collecting and using data for training NLP models.
By following these principles, we can develop NLP models that are fair, safe, and explainable, fostering trust and unlocking the true potential of NLP to benefit everyone. Remember, responsible development is a shared responsibility, and our choices today will shape the future of NLP and its impact on the world.

8.3 The Expanding Applications of NLP Transformers

The emergence of NLP Transformers has sparked a wave of innovation, transforming how machines understand and process human language. These powerful models are finding applications in a vast array of domains, revolutionizing industries and shaping the future of human-computer interaction.

1. Redefining Search and Information Retrieval:

Search engines are leveraging NLP Transformers to deliver more relevant and nuanced search results. By understanding the intent behind a user's query and the relationships between words, Transformers can surface more meaningful information and improve the overall search experience.

Additionally, NLP Transformers are being used to develop intelligent chatbots that can answer user questions in a comprehensive and conversational way. This can be invaluable for customer service applications or information retrieval tasks in various domains.

2. Transforming Machine Translation:

Machine translation has witnessed significant advancements with NLP Transformers. These models can capture the intricacies of language, including idioms and cultural nuances, leading to more accurate and natural-sounding translations.

This paves the way for seamless communication across language barriers, boosting global collaboration and information sharing across different cultures.

3. Powering the Future of Content Creation:

NLP Transformers are making waves in the content creation realm. They can be used for tasks like text summarization, automatically generating concise summaries of lengthy documents or articles.

Additionally, these models can be employed for content generation, assisting writers with tasks like brainstorming ideas, developing outlines, or even creating different creative text formats like poems or scripts.

4. Reimagining Social Media and Online Interactions:

NLP Transformers are being harnessed to improve social media experiences. They can be used for sentiment analysis, identifying positive or negative sentiment in user posts, which can aid in content moderation and improve overall user experience.

NLP Transformers can also personalize social media feeds by understanding user preferences and interests, leading to a more engaging and relevant online experience.

5. Driving Advancements in Scientific Research:

NLP Transformers are finding applications in scientific research domains. They can be used to analyze vast amounts of scientific literature, summarizing key findings and uncovering hidden relationships between different research areas.

This can significantly accelerate scientific progress by facilitating efficient literature review and knowledge discovery.

Beyond these examples, NLP Transformers hold immense potential for various other applications, including:

Automated customer service chatbots
Smart assistants and virtual companions
Enhanced accessibility tools for visually impaired users
Automatic document classification and organization
Spam and malware detection

As NLP Transformer technology continues to evolve, we can expect even more groundbreaking applications to emerge, transforming the way we interact with language and information technology in the years to come. However, it's crucial to ensure responsible development and deployment of these powerful models, considering potential biases and ethical implications to maximize their positive impact on society.